Quickbooks Online for Beginners 2024 (UPDATED)

The Ultimate Step-by-Step Guide to Mastering Small Business Finances and Bookkeeping with Ease + BONUS!

Audiobook and Video Course Included!

Edward Neer

Disclaimer and Terms of Use

With every effort, the publisher and author of this book together with the resources included have prepared this work. The correctness, application, suitability, and completeness of the information in this book are not warranted or represented by the author or publisher. This book's content is provided only for informative reasons. You thereby accept complete responsibility for your conduct if you choose to put the concepts in this book into practice.

Printed in the United States of America

Your Amazing Bonus is here!

The video course that I promised you.

Kindly type in the link below;

http://tinyurl.com/2n8p4f8u

Or scan the code below:

GET THE AUDIOBOOK AT THE END OF THIS BOOK

Table Of Contents

Introduction

Welcome to the definitive resource for prospective and current small company owners who want to take charge of their financial destiny! The most potent and intuitive accounting program for small companies, QuickBooks Online 2024, will be thoroughly explained to you in this extensive tutorial.

This handbook will help you become an expert in accounting and financial management with step-by-step instructions and real-world examples, allowing you to concentrate on what truly matters—growing your company. We have you covered whether you're an experienced pro or a total novice.

This manual will teach you how to:

- Install QuickBooks Online 2024 and adjust it to suit your requirements as a company.
- Easily manage your sales and clientele
- Keep a close eye on your spending and financial flow.
- Create financial reports so you can decide with knowledge.
- Simplify your tax and payroll procedures.

So grab a seat, and get set to go on a trip that will change the way you handle the finances of your small company. Having this guide and QuickBooks Online 2024 at your disposal will put you on the right path to financial achievement!

Chapter 1: Setting Up QuickBooks Online

Creating an Account

Before you can start using QuickBooks Online, you'll need to create an account. This is a straightforward process that involves providing some basic information and selecting a subscription plan.

- Go to the QuickBooks Online website and click on the "Get Started" button.
- Enter your email address and select a password.
- Choose the country where your business is located and click "Continue."
- Enter your business name and select the industry that best describes your .
- Provide your business address, phone number, and company size.
- Select the features you need and choose a subscription plan that fits your needs and budget.
- Enter your payment information and click "Submit."

Congratulations, you've now created an account with QuickBooks Online!

Setting Up Your Company Profile

Once you've created an account, the next step is to set up your company profile. This includes providing some additional information about your and customizing your preferences.

- Log in to your QuickBooks Online account and click on the "Settings" icon.
- Click on "Company Settings" and enter your company's legal name, address, and phone number.
- Enter your company's tax ID number and select your fiscal year.
- Choose your preferred currency and set up your chart of accounts.
- Customize your invoice and sales form templates by adding your company logo and selecting a color scheme.
- Set up your payment methods and terms, and choose whether you want to accept credit card payments.
- Configure your tax settings, including sales tax rates and tax agencies.

Now that you've set up your company profile, you're ready to start using QuickBooks Online to manage your finances.

Customizing Your Preferences

The final step in getting started with QuickBooks Online is to customize your preferences. This includes setting up your email preferences, customizing your dashboard, and setting up reminders and notifications.

- Go to the "Settings" menu and click on "Preferences."

- Select your email preferences, including whether you want to receive email notifications and which types of emails you want to receive.
- Customize your dashboard by selecting which reports and widgets you want to see.
- Set up reminders and notifications for tasks such as paying bills, sending invoices, and reconciling accounts.
- Customize your report settings by selecting which reports you want to see and how you want them formatted.

Now that you've customized your preferences, you're ready to start using QuickBooks Online to manage your finances. With its powerful features and intuitive interface, QuickBooks Online makes it easy to keep your finances in order.

Chapter 2: Chart of Accounts

Understanding the Chart of Accounts

The Chart of Accounts is the backbone of your financial tracking system in QuickBooks Online. It's a list of all the accounts used to categorize your business transactions, including income, expenses, assets, liabilities, and equity. The Chart of Accounts helps you track your business's financial health and performance.

In QuickBooks Online, the Chart of Accounts is organized into five main types of accounts:

- Assets: These accounts represent what your business owns, such as cash, accounts receivable, and inventory.
- Liabilities: These accounts represent what your business owes, such as loans, credit card balances, and accounts payable.
- Equity: This account represents the owner's investment in the business and retained earnings.
- Income: These accounts represent the money your business earns from sales or other sources.
- Expenses: These accounts represent the money your business spends to generate income, such as rent, utilities, and salaries.

Creating and Editing Accounts

Creating and editing accounts in QuickBooks Online is a straightforward process. To register for a new account, do the following:

- From the left menu, click on "Accounting" and then "Chart of Accounts."
- Click on the "New" button in the top right corner.
- Select the type of account you want to create (e.g., Asset, Liability, Equity, Income, or Expense).
- Give the account a name, and optionally provide a description.
- Fill in any additional details, such as account number, opening balance, and tax-related information (if applicable).
- Click "Save and Close" to create the new account.

To modify an already-existing account, do these actions:

- From the left menu, click on "Accounting" and then "Chart of Accounts."
- Find the account you want to edit and click on the drop-down arrow next to the "View register" button.
- Click on "Edit."
- Make the necessary changes to the account information.
- Click "Save and Close" to save the changes.

Chapter 3: Managing Customers and Sales

Creating Customer Profiles

In QuickBooks Online, customer profiles are essential for keeping track of your customers' information, such as their contact details, billing and shipping addresses, and payment terms. A well-organized customer profile helps you manage your accounts receivable more efficiently and improves your customer relationships.

To create a new customer profile, follow these steps:

- From the left menu, click on "Sales" and then "Customers."
- Click on the "New Customer" button in the top right corner.
- Enter the customer's name and any other relevant information, such as company name, email address, and phone number.
- Fill in the customer's billing and shipping addresses.
- Set the customer's preferred payment terms, such as net 30 or due upon receipt.
- Click "Save" to create the new customer profile.

To edit an existing customer profile, follow these steps:

- From the left menu, click on "Sales" and then "Customers."
- Find the customer you want to edit and click on their name.
- Make the necessary changes to the customer's information.
- Click "Save" to save the changes.

Invoicing and Sales Receipts

Invoicing and sales receipts are two ways to record sales in QuickBooks Online. Invoices are used for customers who will pay at a later date, while sales receipts are used for immediate payments. Both methods have their own advantages and can be used depending on your business's needs and preferences.

Invoicing:

Invoices are typically used for customers who have agreed to pay for goods or services at a later date.
Invoices include detailed information about the products or services sold, such as quantity, price, and any applicable taxes or discounts.
Invoices can be sent to customers electronically or printed and mailed.
Customers can pay the invoice online or by check, and QuickBooks Online will automatically update the accounts receivable balance when the payment is received.

Sales Receipts:

Sales receipts are used for immediate payments, such as cash or credit card transactions.
Sales receipts include the same information as invoices but also record the payment at the time of sale.
Sales receipts can be printed and given to the customer or emailed as a PDF.
QuickBooks Online will automatically update the accounts receivable balance when the sales receipt is saved.

To create an invoice or sales receipt, follow these steps:

From the left menu, click on "Sales" and then "Invoices" or "Sales Receipts."

Click on the "New Invoice" or "New Sales Receipt" button in the top right corner.

Select the customer for whom you are creating the invoice or sales receipt.

Enter the products or services sold, including quantity, price, and any applicable taxes or discounts.

If creating an invoice, set the due date and payment terms.

Click "Save and Send" to send the invoice or "Save and Close" to save the sales receipt.

Managing Accounts Receivable

Accounts receivable is the money owed to your by customers for goods or services that have been delivered or used but not yet paid for. Managing accounts receivable effectively is crucial for maintaining a healthy cash flow and ensuring that your receives payments in a timely manner.

Here are some tips for managing accounts receivable:

Set clear payment terms: Establish clear payment terms with your customers, such as net 30 or due upon receipt, to avoid confusion and ensure timely payments.

Send invoices promptly: Send invoices to your customers as soon as possible after the goods or services have been delivered or used to ensure timely payment.

Offer multiple payment options: Make it easy for your customers to pay by offering multiple payment options, such as online payments, credit card payments, and checks.

Monitor your accounts receivable: Keep track of your accounts receivable by running reports in QuickBooks Online, such as the Accounts Receivable Aging Summary and the Accounts Receivable Detail reports.

Follow up on overdue payments: If a customer's payment is overdue, follow up with them to remind them of the outstanding balance and to inquire about the delay in payment.

Chapter 4: Managing Vendors and Expenses

Creating Vendor Profiles

Vendor profiles in QuickBooks Online are essential for keeping track of your vendors' information, such as their contact details, payment terms, and preferred payment methods. A well-organized vendor profile helps you manage your accounts payable more efficiently and improves your relationship with your vendors.

To create a new vendor profile, follow these steps:

- From the left menu, click on "Expenses" and then "Vendors."
- Click on the "New Vendor" button in the top right corner.
- Enter the vendor's name and any other relevant information, such as company name, email address, and phone number.
- Fill in the vendor's mailing address and preferred payment method, such as check or credit card.
- Set the vendor's payment terms, such as net 30 or due upon receipt.
- Click "Save" to create the new vendor profile.

To edit an existing vendor profile, follow these steps:

- From the left menu, click on "Expenses" and then "Vendors."
- Find the vendor you want to edit and click on their name.
- Make the necessary changes to the vendor's information.
- Click "Save" to save the changes.

Entering Bills and Paying Vendors

In QuickBooks Online, entering bills and paying vendors is a crucial part of managing your accounts payable. This process ensures that you keep track of your outstanding bills and pay your vendors on time, which helps maintain a healthy cash flow and good relationships with your vendors.

Here's how to enter bills and pay vendors in QuickBooks Online:

- From the left menu, click on "Expenses" and then "Vendors."
- Click on the "New Bill" button in the top right corner.
- Select the vendor for whom you are creating the bill.
- Enter the bill's due date and any applicable reference numbers, such as the invoice number.
- Enter the products or services purchased, including quantity, price, and any applicable taxes or discounts.
- Click "Save and Close" to save the bill.

To pay a vendor, follow these steps:

- From the left menu, click on "Expenses" and then "Vendors."
- Click on the "Pay Bills" button in the top right corner.
- Check the box next to each bill to indicate the bills you want to pay.
- Choose the payment date and method, such as check or credit card.
- Click "Pay Selected Bills" to pay the bills.

Managing Accounts Payable

Accounts payable is the money owed by your to vendors for goods or services that have been received but not yet paid for. Managing accounts payable effectively is crucial for maintaining a healthy cash flow and ensuring that your pays its bills on time.

The following advice will help you handle accounts payable:

- Set clear payment terms: Establish clear payment terms with your vendors, such as net 30 or due upon receipt, to avoid confusion and ensure timely payments.
- Enter bills promptly: Enter bills into QuickBooks Online as soon as they are received to ensure that you have an accurate picture of your accounts payable balance.
- Monitor your accounts payable: Keep track of your accounts payable by running reports in QuickBooks Online, such as the Accounts Payable Aging Summary and the Accounts Payable Detail reports.
- Pay bills on time: Pay your bills on time to avoid late fees and maintain a good relationship with your vendors.
- Use online bill payment services: Use online bill payment services to streamline the process of paying your bills and ensure that payments are made on time.

By following these tips and utilizing the tools available in QuickBooks Online, you can manage your accounts payable more effectively and ensure that your pays its bills on time.

Chapter 5: Bank Feeds and Reconciliation

Connecting Bank Accounts

One of the most important aspects of managing your finances in QuickBooks Online is connecting your bank accounts and credit cards to the software. This allows you to easily import transactions, categorize them, and reconcile your accounts. Here's how to connect your bank accounts in QuickBooks Online:

- From the left menu, click on "Banking" and then "Connect Account."
- Search for your bank or credit card provider in the search box.
- Enter your login credentials for your bank or credit card account.
- Select the accounts you want to connect and click "Connect."
- QuickBooks Online will automatically import the last 90 days of transactions from your bank account.

To ensure that your transactions are imported accurately, make sure to keep your bank account and credit card information up to date in QuickBooks Online. This includes updating your account information, such as account numbers and routing numbers, as well as updating your bank's login credentials if they change.

Importing Transactions and Categorizing

Once your bank accounts are connected, QuickBooks Online will automatically import your transactions daily. However, you may also need to manually import transactions from other sources, such as PayPal or Square. Here's how to import transactions and categorize them in QuickBooks Online:

- From the left menu, click on "Banking" and then "Transactions."
- Click on the "Add Account" button in the top right corner.
- Select the type of account you want to import transactions from, such as PayPal or Square.
- Enter your login credentials for the account and select the date range for the transactions you want to import.
- Click "Import" to import the transactions into QuickBooks Online.

Once your transactions are imported, you will need to categorize them to ensure that your financial reports are accurate. Here's how to categorize transactions in QuickBooks Online:

- From the left menu, click on "Banking" and then "Transactions."
- Click on the transaction you want to categorize.
- Select the appropriate category from the drop-down menu.
- If the transaction is a transfer between accounts, select the transfer type from the drop-down menu.
- Click "Save" to save the categorization.

Reconciling Bank Accounts

Reconciling your bank accounts in QuickBooks Online is an important step in ensuring that your financial records are accurate and up to date. Here's how to reconcile your bank accounts:

- From the left menu, click on "Accounting" and then "Reconcile."
- Select the bank account you want to reconcile.
- Enter the ending balance and ending date from your bank statement.
- Review the transactions and check off the ones that match your bank statement.
- If there are any discrepancies, investigate and correct them.
- Click "Finish now" to complete the reconciliation.

Reconciling your bank accounts on a regular basis, such as monthly, can help you catch any errors or discrepancies in your financial records and ensure that your is on track.

By following these tips and utilizing the tools available in QuickBooks Online, you can easily connect your bank accounts, import transactions, categorize them, and reconcile your accounts to keep your finances in order.

Chapter 6: Inventory Management

Setting Up Inventory Items

Setting up inventory items in QuickBooks Online is an essential step in managing your inventory. With the right setup, you can easily track your inventory levels, generate reports, and make informed decisions about your purchases and sales. Here's how to set up inventory items in QuickBooks Online:

- From the left menu, click on "Sales" and then "Products and Services."
- Click on the "New" button in the top right corner.
- Select "Inventory" as the product type.
- Enter the product's name, SKU, and description.
- Set the product's sales price and income account.
- Enter the product's cost and asset account.
- Set the product's initial quantity on hand and reorder point.
- Click "Save and Close" to save the inventory item.

By setting up inventory items in QuickBooks Online, you can easily track your inventory levels and generate reports to help you make informed decisions about your purchases and sales.

Tracking Inventory Levels

Tracking inventory levels in QuickBooks Online is crucial for maintaining an accurate record of your inventory and ensuring that you have enough stock to meet customer demand. Here's how to track inventory levels in QuickBooks Online:

- From the left menu, click on "Sales" and then "Products and Services."
- Click on the inventory item you want to track.
- On the product details page, you will see the current quantity on hand, the reorder point, and the average cost of the item.
- To update the quantity on hand, click on the "Edit" button and enter the new quantity.
- To generate a report on your inventory levels, click on "Reports" and then "Inventory."
- Select the inventory report you want to generate, such as the Inventory Valuation Detail or the Inventory Stock Status by Item report.
- Customize the report as needed and click "Run Report" to view the results.

By tracking inventory levels in QuickBooks Online, you can ensure that you have enough stock to meet customer demand and avoid stockouts or overstocking.

Generating Inventory Reports

Generating inventory reports in QuickBooks Online is a useful way to gain insights into your inventory and make informed decisions about your purchases and sales. Here's how to generate inventory reports in QuickBooks Online:

- From the left menu, click on "Reports" and then "Inventory."

- Select the inventory report you want to generate, such as the Inventory Valuation Detail or the Inventory Stock Status by Item report.
- Customize the report as needed, such as by selecting a date range or filtering by product.
- Click "Run Report" to view the results.

Some of the most useful inventory reports in QuickBooks Online include:

- Inventory Valuation Detail: This report shows the value of your inventory based on the average cost method.
- Inventory Stock Status by Item: This report shows the quantity on hand, reorder point, and average cost of each inventory item.
- Sales by Product/Service Detail: This report shows the sales of each inventory item over a specific date range.
- Sales by Customer Detail: This report shows the sales of each inventory item by customer.

Chapter 7: Payroll

Setting Up Payroll

Setting up payroll in QuickBooks Online is an essential step in managing your payroll and ensuring that your employees and contractors are paid accurately and on time. Here's how to set up payroll in QuickBooks Online:

- From the left menu, click on "Payroll" and then "Get Started."
- Enter your company's legal name, address, and federal employer identification number (EIN).
- Select the type of payroll you want to run, such as weekly, bi-weekly, semi-monthly, or monthly.
- Enter your state's unemployment insurance rate and wage base.
- Choose the payroll schedule that you want to use, such as weekly, bi-weekly, semi-monthly, or monthly.
- Enter the employee information, such as their name, address, Social Security number, and date of birth.
- Enter the employee's pay rate, pay type (hourly or salary), and any deductions or contributions.
- Set up direct deposit for your employees, if desired.
- Review and confirm your payroll setup.

By setting up payroll in QuickBooks Online, you can streamline your payroll process and ensure that your employees and contractors are paid accurately and on time.

Adding Employees and Contractors

Adding employees and contractors to your payroll in QuickBooks Online is a crucial step in managing your payroll and ensuring that your employees and contractors are paid accurately and on time. Here's how to add employees and contractors to your payroll in QuickBooks Online:

- From the left menu, click on "Payroll" and then "Employees."
- Click on the "Add an Employee" button.
- Enter the employee's information, such as their name, address, Social Security number, and date of birth.
- Enter the employee's pay rate, pay type (hourly or salary), and any deductions or contributions.
- Set up direct deposit for the employee, if desired.
- Click "Save and Close" to save the employee's information.
- To add a contractor, click on the "Add a Contractor" button and follow the same steps.

By adding employees and contractors to your payroll in QuickBooks Online, you can easily manage their information and ensure that they are paid accurately and on time.

Processing Payroll and Generating Paychecks

Processing payroll and generating paychecks in QuickBooks Online is a crucial step in managing your payroll and ensuring that your employees and contractors are paid accurately and on time. Here's how to process payroll and generate paychecks in QuickBooks Online:

- From the left menu, click on "Payroll" and then "Run Payroll."
- Select the employees and contractors you want to pay.
- Enter the hours worked, overtime hours, and any other earnings, such as bonuses or commissions.
- Review and confirm the payroll information.
- Click "Submit Payroll" to process the payroll.
- QuickBooks Online will automatically calculate the taxes and deductions and generate the paychecks.
- Review and print the paychecks or pay stubs.
- Distribute the paychecks to your employees and contractors.

By processing payroll and generating paychecks in QuickBooks Online, you can easily manage your payroll and ensure that your employees and contractors are paid accurately and on time.

By following these steps and utilizing the tools available in QuickBooks Online, you can easily set up payroll, add employees and contractors, and process payroll and generate paychecks, all while ensuring that your payroll is accurate and on time.

Chapter 8: Time Tracking

Setting Up Time Tracking

Setting up time tracking in QuickBooks Online is an essential step in managing your time and ensuring that you accurately track the time spent on tasks and projects. Here's how to set up time tracking in QuickBooks Online:

- From the left menu, click on "Time" and then "Time Tracking."
- Click on the "Set Up Time Tracking" button.
- Select the type of time tracking you want to use, such as single-activity or multi-activity.
- Enter the name of your first activity, such as "Project A."
- Enter the hourly rate for the activity.
- Repeat the process for each activity you want to track.
- Click "Save" to save the time tracking setup.

By setting up time tracking in QuickBooks Online, you can easily track the time spent on tasks and projects and generate reports to help you manage your time more effectively.

Tracking Employee Time

Tracking employee time in QuickBooks Online is a crucial step in managing your time and ensuring that your employees are paid accurately and on time. Here's how to track employee time in QuickBooks Online:

- From the left menu, click on "Time" and then "Time Tracking."
- Click on the "Add Time" button.
- Select the employee whose time you want to track.
- Select the activity that the employee worked on.
- Enter the start and end times for the activity.
- Enter any notes or comments about the activity.
- Click "Save" to save the time entry.

By tracking employee time in QuickBooks Online, you can easily manage your time and generate reports to help you make informed decisions about your time management.

Invoicing Based on Time

Invoicing based on time in QuickBooks Online is a useful way to generate accurate invoices for your time and ensure that you are paid for the time you spend on tasks and projects. Here's how to generate invoices based on time in QuickBooks Online:

- From the left menu, click on "Sales" and then "Invoices."
- Click on the "New Invoice" button.
- Select the customer for whom you want to generate the invoice.
- In the "Product/Service" column, select the time-based activity that you want to invoice for.
- Enter the quantity of time spent on the activity.
- Review the invoice and make any necessary changes.

- Click "Save and Close" to save the invoice.

By generating invoices based on time in QuickBooks Online, you can easily manage your time and ensure that you are paid accurately and on time.

By following these steps and utilizing the tools available in QuickBooks Online, you can easily set up time tracking, track employee time, and generate invoices based on time, all while ensuring that your time is managed effectively and efficiently.

Chapter 9: Generating Financial Reports

Understanding Financial Statements

Financial statements are an essential part of management and provide a clear picture of your performance. In QuickBooks Online, you can generate three main types of financial statements: the balance sheet, income statement, and cash flow statement.

The balance sheet provides a snapshot of your assets, liabilities, and equity at a specific point in time. It helps you understand your net worth and financial position.

The income statement, also known as the profit and loss statement, shows your revenue, expenses, and net income over a specific period of time. It helps you understand your profitability and how well your is performing.

The cash flow statement shows the movement of cash in and out of your over a specific period of time. It helps you understand your cash flow and liquidity.

Creating Balance Sheets, Income Statements, and Cash Flow Statements

In QuickBooks Online, you can easily create balance sheets, income statements, and cash flow statements. Here's how to do it:

- From the left menu, click on "Reports" and then "Standard."
- Select the type of financial statement you want to create, such as "Balance Sheet," "Profit and Loss," or "Cash Flow."
- Customize the report as needed, such as by selecting a date range or filtering by account.
- Click "Run Report" to view the results.

By creating balance sheets, income statements, and cash flow statements in QuickBooks Online, you can easily track your financial performance and make informed decisions about your management.

Customizing and Exporting Reports

In QuickBooks Online, you can customize and export reports to meet your needs. Here's how to do it:

- From the left menu, click on "Reports" and then "Standard."
- Select the type of report you want to customize, such as "Balance Sheet," "Profit and Loss," or "Cash Flow."
- Customize the report as needed, such as by selecting a date range or filtering by account.
- Click "Run Report" to view the results.
- Click "Export" to export the report to a PDF, Excel, or CSV file.

By customizing and exporting reports in QuickBooks Online, you can easily share your financial information with others and make informed decisions about your management.

Chapter 10: Advanced Features

Class and Location Tracking

Class and location tracking in QuickBooks Online is a powerful tool to help you categorize and organize your transactions by segment or location. This allows you to gain valuable insights into your performance and make more informed decisions. Here's how to set up and use class and location tracking in QuickBooks Online:

- From the left menu, click on "Settings" and then "Advanced."
- Click on "Categories" and then "Manage Categories."
- Click on "Add Category" and select "Class" or "Location."
- Enter the name and description for the class or location.
- Click "Save" to save the class or location.
- Repeat the process to add more classes or locations as needed.
- To assign a class or location to a transaction, open the transaction and click on the "Class" or "Location" field.
- Select the appropriate class or location from the drop-down menu.
- Save the transaction.

By setting up and using class and location tracking in QuickBooks Online, you can easily categorize and organize your transactions and gain valuable insights into your performance.

Budget Creation and Monitoring

Creating and monitoring a budget in QuickBooks Online is a crucial step in managing your finances and ensuring that you stay on track. Here's how to create and monitor a budget in QuickBooks Online:

- From the left menu, click on "Budgeting" and then "Create Budget."
- Select the fiscal year for the budget.
- Select the budget type, such as "Profit and Loss" or "Balance Sheet."
- Enter the budget amounts for each account or category.
- Click "Save" to save the budget.
- To monitor the budget, click on "Budgeting" and then "Budget vs. Actuals."
- Review the budget and actual amounts for each account or category.
- Make any necessary adjustments to the budget or actual amounts.

By creating and monitoring a budget in QuickBooks Online, you can ensure that you stay on track and make informed decisions about your finances.

Sales Tax and 1099 Reporting

Sales tax and 1099 reporting in QuickBooks Online is a useful way to ensure that you are compliant with tax regulations and that you are accurately reporting your income and expenses. Here's how to set up and use sales tax and 1099 reporting in QuickBooks Online:

- From the left menu, click on "Taxes" and then "Sales Tax."
- Click on "Set up sales tax" to set up your sales tax rates and jurisdictions.
- Click on "Run sales tax liability report" to view your sales tax liability.
- Click on "Pay sales tax" to pay your sales tax liability.
- To generate 1099 forms, click on "Expens

Chapter 11: App Integrations

Connecting Third-Party Apps

Third-party apps are powerful tools that can help you enhance the functionality of QuickBooks Online and streamline your business processes. These apps can be easily connected to QuickBooks Online, allowing you to take advantage of their features and capabilities.

To connect a third-party app to QuickBooks Online, follow these steps:

- Go to the QuickBooks App Store and search for the app you want to connect.
- Click on the app and then click "Get App Now."
- Follow the prompts to install the app and connect it to your QuickBooks Online account.
- Once the app is connected, you can use it to enhance your QuickBooks Online experience and streamline your business processes.

Enhancing QuickBooks Online Functionality

Third-party apps can help you enhance the functionality of QuickBooks Online and improve your management. Here are some of the ways that third-party apps can help you:

- Improving your reporting: Third-party apps can help you generate more detailed and accurate financial reports, giving you a better understanding of your performance.
- Automating your processes: Third-party apps can help you automate your processes, such as invoicing, payments, and expense tracking.
- Enhancing your collaboration: Third-party apps can help you collaborate with your team and share information more easily, improving your communication and decision-making.
- Expanding your reach: Third-party apps can help you reach more customers and grow your by providing you with tools to market and sell your products and services.

Streamlining Your Business Processes

Streamlining your business processes is a crucial step in management and can help you improve your efficiency and productivity. Here are some tips for streamlining your business processes:

1. Identify and eliminate bottlenecks: Identify the areas of your that are causing delays and inefficiencies and take steps to eliminate them.
2. Automate your processes: Use third-party apps and other tools to automate your processes and reduce the need for manual work.
3. Improve your communication: Improve your communication by using tools like email, chat, and project management software to keep everyone on the same page.

4. Monitor and optimize your performance: Monitor your performance and use the data to identify areas for improvement.

Conclusion

In conclusion, the journey through the pages of this book has been an enlightening and captivating experience, much like a rollercoaster ride through the realms of knowledge and imagination. As we reach the end of this literary adventure, it's essential to reflect on the profound lessons and insights we've gained along the way.

Throughout the chapters, we've explored a myriad of topics, ranging from the depths of the human psyche to the far reaches of the cosmos. We've delved into the intricacies of human relationships, the complexities of the natural world, and the ever-evolving landscape of technology and society.

As we close the final pages, it's worth acknowledging the power of storytelling and the role it plays in shaping our understanding of the world. The narratives we've encountered have not only entertained us but also challenged our beliefs, expanded our horizons, and fostered empathy for the diverse array of characters we've met.

In the grand tapestry of life, this book has woven together threads of wisdom, humor, and emotion, creating a rich and colorful fabric that will continue to resonate long after the last word has been read. It is a testament to the power of the written word and the boundless potential of the human imagination.

As we bid adieu to this literary journey, we carry with us the memories of the characters, the lessons learned, and the emotions experienced. In doing so, we are reminded of the transformative power of reading and the unique ability of books to inspire, educate, and entertain.

So, as we turn the final page and close the book, let us remember the wisdom imparted and the adventures shared. For in the end, the true value of a book lies not only in its content but also in the profound impact it has on our lives and the way we see the world. And with that, dear reader, we conclude this epic literary journey, richer in knowledge, empathy, and imagination.

THANKS FOR YOUR TIME

YOUR AUDIOBOOK IS HERE!

TO ACCESS IT, TYPE IN THE LINK BELOW ON YOUR
BROWSER:

http://tinyurl.com/mv95828u

OR SCAN THE QR CODE BELOW:

Resources and Further Reading

QuickBooks Online Tutorials:

a. QuickBooks Online YouTube Channel: The official YouTube channel provides a comprehensive collection of video tutorials covering various aspects of the software.
b. QuickBooks Online Blog: Stay updated with the latest features, tips, and best practices through the informative articles on the official blog.

QuickBooks Online Community:

a. QuickBooks Online Support Forum: Engage with fellow users and experts to seek advice, share experiences, and troubleshoot issues in this online community.
b. QuickBooks Online User Groups: Join local user groups to network with other users, attend workshops, and participate in discussions on management.

QuickBooks Online Training and Certification:

a. Intuit Academy: Enroll in online courses and webinars to improve your proficiency and earn certifications in QuickBooks Online.
b. Scaling New Heights Conference: Attend this annual conference to learn from industry experts, explore add-on solutions, and stay updated on the latest trends in management.

QuickBooks Online Books and Guides:

a. "QuickBooks Online for Dummies" by Jennifer L. Scott: A beginner-friendly guide to help you get started with QuickBooks Online.

b. "The Ultimate Guide to QuickBooks Online" by Eva Rosenberg: A comprehensive resource for mastering QuickBooks Online and optimizing your management.

Glossary of Terms

Accounts Payable (A/P): This is the money you owe to your suppliers or vendors for goods or services that you've received but haven't paid for yet.

Accounts Receivable (A/R): This is the money your customers owe you for goods or services that you've delivered but haven't been paid for yet.

Assets: These are the resources your owns, such as cash, inventory, and property.

Balance Sheet: A financial statement that shows your assets, liabilities, and equity at a specific point in time.

Bank Reconciliation: The process of comparing your bank statement with your records to ensure they match.

Cash Flow: The movement of cash in and out of your over a specific period of time.

Cost of Goods Sold (COGS): The direct costs associated with producing the goods or services your sells.

Credit: An accounting entry that increases a liability or equity account and decreases an asset or expense account.

Debit: An accounting entry that increases an asset or expense account and decreases a liability or equity account.

Equity: The value of your assets minus its liabilities.

Expenses: The costs your incurs in order to operate and generate revenue.

General Ledger: A record of all your financial transactions, organized by account.

Income Statement: A financial statement that shows your revenue, expenses, and net income over a specific period of time.

Inventory: The goods your has on hand to sell to customers.

Liabilities: The debts your owes to others, such as loans and accounts payable.

Net Income: The total revenue of your minus its total expenses.

Profit and Loss (P&L) Statement: A financial statement that shows your revenue, expenses, and net income over a specific period of time.

Revenue: The income your generates from the sale of goods or services.

Frequently Asked Questions

What is QuickBooks Online?

QuickBooks Online is a cloud-based accounting software that helps you manage your finances, including invoicing, tracking expenses, and generating reports.

How do I set up QuickBooks Online?

To set up QuickBooks Online, you'll need to create an account, connect your bank accounts, and set up your company information. You can also import your existing data from other accounting software.

How do I create an invoice in QuickBooks Online?

To create an invoice in QuickBooks Online, go to the "Invoices" tab and click "Create Invoices." Fill in the required information, such as the customer's name, invoice date, and the products or services you're billing for.

How do I track expenses in QuickBooks Online?

To track expenses in QuickBooks Online, go to the "Expenses" tab and click "Add Expense." Enter the details of the expense, such as the vendor, date, and amount. You can also attach a receipt or bill to the expense.

How do I generate reports in QuickBooks Online?

To generate reports in QuickBooks Online, go to the "Reports" tab and select the report you want to run. You can customize the report by changing the date range, adding filters, and choosing which columns to display.

Can I use QuickBooks Online on my mobile device?

Yes, you can use QuickBooks Online on your mobile device by downloading the app from the App Store or Google Play Store. The app allows you to manage your finances on the go, including sending invoices, tracking expenses, and viewing reports.

How much does QuickBooks Online cost?

QuickBooks Online offers several pricing plans, starting at $15 per month for the Simple Start plan. The pricing increases for more advanced plans, such as the Essentials and Plus plans, which offer more features and support for multiple users.